First Women

American Originators

Edited by
Evelyn & Nick Beilenson

Designed by
Darlenedea Lazarte and
Sandra Baenen

PETER PAUPER PRESS, INC.
WHITE PLAINS • NEW YORK

Table of Contents

Susan B. Anthony

First Woman to be honored on an American coin

"The true republic—men, their rights and nothing more; women, their rights and nothing less."

Born 1820, died 1906
Birthplace: Adams, Massachusetts
Education: By her father at home, and at Deborah Moulson's Boarding School
Marital Status/Children: Single. Anthony said: "I never had time" (to get married).
Occupation: Social reformer
Publications: Founded and edited the newspaper *Revolution* (1868-70); *A History of Woman Suffrage* (with Elizabeth Cady Stanton).
Honors: Anthony's likeness appears on the Susan B. Anthony silver dollar. She was elected to the Hall of Fame in 1950.
Footnote: Anthony founded the Daughters of Temperance in 1848. In 1872-73 she challenged the New York election law by casting her vote. A prominent suffragette, Anthony was a leader of the National Woman Suffrage Association (1869-90) and president of the merged National American Woman Suffrage Association (1892-1900).

Jane Addams

First American Woman to win the Nobel Peace Prize

"Private beneficence is totally inadequate to deal with the vast number of the city's disinherited."

Born 1860, died 1935
Birthplace: Cedarville, Illinois
Education: Graduated from Rockford College.
Marital Status/Children: Single
Occupation: Social worker, pacifist
Publications: *Democracy and Social Ethics, Twenty Years at Hull House, Memory,* and many more
Honors: Awarded Nobel Peace Prize in 1931; first woman to receive an honorary degree from Yale.
Footnote: In 1889 Jane Addams founded Hull House, a settlement in the slums of Chicago, to help the poor with their housing, education and labor problems. By 1911, 400 "Hull Houses" had been established. The passage of several social reform bills, such as the Mother's Pension Act and Illinois' first Factory Inspection Act, were due to her initiatives. After World War I, Jane Addams addressed herself exclusively to the cause of peace.

Marian Anderson

First Black Woman to sing solo at the Metropolitan Opera

"There was a time when I was very much interested in applause and the lovely things they said. But now we are interested in singing so that somebody in the audience will leave feeling a little better than when he came."

Born 1902
Birthplace: Philadelphia, Pennsylvania
Education: Graduated from South Philadelphia High School; music school.
Marital Status/Children: Married Orpheus H. Fisher in 1943; no children.
Occupation: Singer, delegate to the UN
Honors: Spingarn Medal, Bok Award, Presidential Medal of Freedom; honorary degrees
Footnote: Marian Anderson has had a distinguished singing career, including a triumphal tour of Europe and a precedent-setting debut at the Metropolitan Opera in 1955. In 1939, when the DAR barred her from Constitution Hall, Eleanor Roosevelt resigned from the DAR and arranged for Miss Anderson to sing at the Lincoln Memorial—where she sang before 75,000 people on Easter Sunday.

Clara Barton

First president and founder of the American Red Cross

"Everybody's business is nobody's business, and nobody's business is my business."

Born 1821, died 1912
Birthplace: Oxford, Massachusetts
Education: Educated at home.
Marital Status/Children: Single
Occupation: Teacher, administrator
Publications: *The Red Cross in Peace and War*
Honors: Medals from many governments
Footnote: During the Civil War Clara Barton distributed food and medical supplies to the wounded. She carried first aid supplies to camps, battlefields and hospitals via mule train. In 1869, "the Angel of the Battlefield" went to Europe to recuperate from a breakdown. Here she heard of the International Committee of the Red Cross and launched a campaign to organize the American Red Cross and to persuade the United States to accept the Geneva Convention on the treatment of war wounded. The American Red Cross was formed in 1881 and the US signed the Convention in 1882.

Edna Rudolph Beilenson

First Woman president of American Institute of Graphic Arts

"We have placed beautiful books in the hands of millions of readers. That's a bigger contribution than I ever could have made writing that great American novel."

Born 1909, died 1981
Birthplace: New York City
Education: Hunter College (BA)
Marital Status/Children: Married Peter Beilenson in 1930, had 3 children. A second marriage, to Joseph E. Barmack, ended in divorce.
Occupation: Publisher, printer
Honors: Who's Who Outstanding Woman of the Year in Business (1967); President, Goudy Society; Frederic W. Goudy Award, Rochester Institute of Technology (1980).
Footnote: Beilenson was co-publisher of Peter Pauper Press from 1932-62 and sole publisher, after her husband's death, from 1962-81. From 1958-1960 Edna Beilenson was the first woman president of the AIGA, publishing industry typographical trade association. She published or co-published 500 fine books "at prices even a pauper could afford."

9

Dr. Elizabeth Blackwell

First Woman in the United States to qualify as a doctor

"Medicine is so broad a field, so closely interwoven with general interests, dealing as it does with all ages, sexes, and classes, and yet of so personal a character in its individual applications, that it must be regarded as one of those great departments of work in which the cooperation of men and women is needed to fulfill all its requirements."

Born 1821, died 1910
Birthplace: Bristol, England
Education: Geneva Medical School
Marital Status/Children: Single, adopted Katharine Barry in 1854.
Occupation: Educator and physician; professor of Gynaecology at London School of Medicine.
Publications: *Pioneer Work in Opening the Medical Profession to Women,* and many other books and essays
Footnote: Blackwell opened a private clinic which became the New York Infirmary for Women and Children, the first hospital with an all-woman staff and where female students could get clinical experience.

Margaret Bourke-White

First Woman photo-journalist; First Woman to be accredited as a war correspondent to the US Army

"If my sister or I took one of those school examinations where you are required to answer only 10 questions out of 12, Mother's comment on hearing this would be, 'I hope you chose the hardest ones.' Reject the easy path. Do it the hard way."

Born 1906, died 1971
Birthplace: New York City
Education: Graduated from Cornell, 1927.
Marital Status/Children: Bourke-White had brief marriages to Everett Chapman (1925-26) and to writer Erskine Caldwell (1939-42). Both ended in divorce.
Occupation: Photo-journalist
Publications: *You Have Seen Their Faces, Eyes on Russia, A Study of the New India, Portrait of Myself,* and others
Footnote: Bourke-White was the first U.S. reporter into Russia after the Revolution and is noted for her photographs of the Great Depression, World War II, and the liberation of Buchenwald Concentration Camp. She served *Life Magazine* as photo-journalist and editor for 33 years.

Amelia Jenks Bloomer

**First Woman to own and publish
a newspaper**

*"The costume of women should be suited to her
wants and necessities. It should conduce at
once to her health, comfort, and usefulness;
and, while it should not fail also to conduce to
her personal adornment, it should make that
end of secondary importance."*

Born 1818, died 1894
Birthplace: Homer, New York
Education: Local schools
Marital Status/Children: Married Dexter C.
Bloomer in 1840.
Occupation: Editor, social reformer,
postmistress
Footnote: Bloomer was the editor and
founder of the *Lily,* a newspaper which
advocated women's rights and temperance.
Under a short skirt she wore full cut pants,
which came to be called "bloomers," a bold
statement of her interest in the dress reform
movement. Ironically, Bloomer's unorthodox
dress often distracted attention from her
social reform efforts.

Antoinette L. Brown

**First Woman in the United States
to be ordained a minister**

*"There were angry men confronting me and I
caught the flashing of defiant eyes, but above
me and within me, there was a spirit stronger
than them all."*

Born 1825, died 1921
Birthplace: Henrietta, New York
Education: Oberlin College, Oberlin
Seminary
Marital Status/Children: married Samuel
Blackwell in 1856, mother of 7 children.
Occupation: Congregational and Unitarian
minister, suffragette
Publications: Wrote 10 books.
Honors: Honorary doctor of divinity from
Oberlin (1908)
Footnote: Brown was the classmate and
sister-in-law of Lucy Stone and Elizabeth
and Emily Blackwell, all prominent women
in their own right. She was the minister of a
parish in South Butler, New York, for one
year, after which she preached and lectured
throughout the country at different times of
her life.

Pearl S. Buck

First American Woman to win the Nobel Prize for Literature

"It is not healthy when a nation lives within a nation, as colored Americans are living inside America. A nation cannot live confident of its tomorrow if its refugees are among its own citizens."

Born 1892, died 1973
Birthplace: Hillsboro, West Virginia
Education: Randolph-Macon Women's College (BA); Cornell University (MA)
Marital Status/Children: Married John L. Buck in 1917, divorced; married Richard Walsh in 1935. Had one natural child and adopted 9 children.
Occupation: Writer, teacher
Honors: Pulitzer Prize for *The Good Earth* (1931); Nobel Prize in Literature (1938); member of the National Institute of Arts and Letters; Yale honorary degree.
Publications: More than 100 books.
Footnote: Pearl Buck's books reflect the fact that she spent much of her life in China. She also founded agencies for adoption of and assistance to Asian-American children.

Hattie Wyatt Caraway

First Woman elected to the US Senate

"After suffrage I just added voting to cooking and sewing."

Born 1878, died 1950
Birthplace: Bakerville, Tennessee
Education: Dickson Academy (BA)
Marital Status/Children: Married Thaddeus Caraway in 1902; 3 sons.
Occupation: Housewife, public official
Footnote: Hattie Caraway, a Democrat, was appointed by the governor of Arkansas to her husband's Senate seat after his death. In a 1932 special election, she was elected unopposed to finish his term. Caraway was re-elected to full terms in 1932 and 1938, before being defeated in 1944 by J. William Fulbright. She was the first woman to chair a Senate committee and the first woman to conduct Senate hearings and preside over Senate sessions. Caraway also served as a member of the Federal Employees' Compensation Commission.

Mary Cassatt

First American Impressionist

"I am independent! I can live alone and I love to work."

Born 1844, died 1926
Birthplace: Allegheny City, Pennsylvania
Education: Schools in Europe; Pennsylvania Academy of the Fine Arts
Marital Status/Children: Single
Occupation: Artist
Footnote: In 1874, Cassatt became a permanent resident of France, where she studied with Degas and exhibited with the Impressionists and alone. A show of her work at the Philadelphia Academy of the Fine Arts in 1876 introduced Impressionism to the United States. Cassatt is noted especially for her etchings, and for her oils and pastels as well. Although she never married, her most famous subjects are mothers and children.

Shirley Chisholm

First Black Woman to be elected to Congress

"Black women are not here to compete or fight with you, brothers. If we have hangups about being male or female, we're not going to be able to use our talents to liberate all of our black people."

Born: 1924
Birthplace: Brooklyn, New York
Education: Brooklyn College; Columbia University (Master's degree)
Marital Status/Children: Married Conrad Chisholm (1949), divorced (1977); married Arthur Hardwick, Jr.
Occupation: Public official, teacher
Publications: *Unbought and Unbossed* (autobiography)
Footnote: After serving as NY State Assemblywoman, Chisholm in 1969 became the first black female elected to the US Congress (where she served until 1983). In 1972 Chisholm pursued the Democratic nomination for President of the United States, receiving 154 delegate votes at the convention. Chisholm has held a professorship at Mount Holyoke College.

18

Dr. Gerty Cori

First American Woman to win a Nobel Prize in the Sciences

"Intellectual integrity, courage, and kindness are still the virtues I admire most."

Born 1896, died 1957
Birthplace: Prague, Czechoslovakia
Education: German University in Prague (MD)
Marital Status/Children: Married Carl Ferdinand Cori in 1920; had one son.
Occupation: Physician, physiologist, biochemist
Publications: Many articles in scientific journals
Honors: 1947 Nobel Prize in physiology and medicine (shared); Garvan Gold Medal; Borden Award
Footnote: Dr. Cori and her husband won the Nobel Prize for their research on carbohydrate metabolism and enzymes. Dr. Cori also served on the Board of the National Science Foundation, was a member of the prestigious National Academy of Sciences, and was professor of biochemistry at Washington University in St. Louis.

Elizabeth Hanford Dole

First Woman to become Secretary of Transportation

"Women share with men the need for personal success, even the taste for power, and no longer are we willing to satisfy those needs through the achievements of surrogates, whether husbands, children or merely role models."

Born 1936
Birthplace: Salisbury, North Carolina
Education: Duke University (BA); Harvard (MA in Education); Harvard Law School (JD)
Marital Status/Children: Married Robert Dole in 1975
Occupation: Lawyer, public official
Honors: Arthur S. Flemming Award for Outstanding Government Service
Footnote: On February 7, 1983, Elizabeth Dole was sworn in as Secretary of Transportation. In the fall of 1987 she resigned to work full time for the Presidential candidacy of her husband, Senator Robert Dole. "I don't think I've set my career aside," she said. "What I'm doing now is playing a substantive role in this process that selects the leader of the free world."

Amelia Earhart

First Woman to fly solo across the Atlantic

"Adventure is worthwhile in itself."

Born 1898, died 1937
Birthplace: Atchison, Kansas
Education: Attended Columbia University
and University of Southern California
Marital Status/Children: Married George
Palmer Putnam in 1931
Occupation: Army nurse, social worker,
aviator, aviation editor
Publications: *20 Hours, 40 Minutes; The Fun
of It; Last Flight*
Footnote: In May, 1932, Earhart flew solo
across the Atlantic, struggling through
stormy weather, the wings of her plane
becoming coated with ice. When Earhart
landed safely in a field in Ireland she
became an immediate international sen-
sation. In 1937 Earhart attempted to fly
around the world, with aviator Fred
Noonan. Radio contact with them was lost
on a hop from New Guinea to Howland
Island and no trace of the plane was ever
discovered.

Mary Baker Eddy

First American Woman to found a major religion

"Matter and death are mortal illusions."

Born 1821, died 1910
Birthplace: Bow, New Hampshire
Education: Ipswich Seminary and private tutors
Marital Status/Children: Married George W. Glover, widowed; married Daniel Patterson, divorced; married Asa G. Eddy.
Occupation: Teacher, writer, founder of Church of Christ, Scientist
Publications: *Christian Science Journal,* which became the *Christian Science Monitor;* many books, including *Science and Health with Key to the Scriptures* (the text book of Christian Science)
Honors: Grand prize and diploma of honor by French government as founder of Christian Science; decorated Officier d'Academie, 1907.
Footnote: Mary Baker Eddy's recovery from ill health by means of spiritual healing led to her founding of Christian Science, based on the theory that the ailments of the body can be cured by mental effort alone in accord with the writings of Jesus.

Susan R. Estrich

First Woman presidential campaign manager

"We've got women everywhere in this campaign. It's not a matter of tokenism. It's not a matter of symbolism. It's done not because we set out to be half and half but because we set out to get the best people, and half of the best people were women."

Born 1952
Birthplace: Lynn, Massachusetts
Education: Wellesley College, (1974); Harvard Law School (JD, 1977)
Marital Status/Children: Married Martin Kaplan in 1986.
Occupation: Law professor, political staffer
Honors: Phi Beta Kappa, Durant Scholar
Footnote: Estrich, on leave from a professorship at Harvard Law School, managed the campaign of Mass. Governor Michael S. Dukakis for the 1988 Democratic presidential nomination. Previously, she held senior staff positions in the Edward Kennedy and Walter Mondale presidential campaigns. She served as executive director of the Democratic National Platform Committee in 1984. Estrich was the first woman president of the Harvard Law Review.

Margaret Fuller

**First American Woman foreign
correspondent**

*"In order that she may be able to give her
hand with dignity, she must be able to stand
alone."*

Born 1810, died 1850
Birthplace: Cambridge, Massachusetts
Education: Private tutoring
Marital Status/Children: Married Marchese
Angelo Ossoli; one son.
Occupation: Editor, educator, literary critic,
correspondent
Publications: *Woman in the Nineteenth
Century* (1845), a pioneering feminist work;
*Papers on Literature and Art; At Home and
Abroad*
Footnote: After teaching, Margaret Fuller
became editor of the transcendentalist
magazine, *The Dial.* Horace Greeley invited
her to become the literary critic for the *New
York Tribune*, and, in 1846, Fuller became
foreign correspondent for the *Tribune.* In
Italy she married, and became deeply
involved in the 1848 Italian Revolution.
Fuller and her husband died in a
shipwreck on their way home to the United
States.

Geraldine A. Ferraro

First Woman nominated as Vice-President by a major party

"I haven't gone through life having things given to me. I had to work for it. So if that makes you tough, yeah, I guess I'm tough."

Born 1935
Birthplace: Newburgh, New York
Education: Marymount College (BA, 1956); Fordham Law School (JD, 1960)
Marital Status/Children: Married John Zaccaro (1960), has two daughters and a son.
Occupation: Attorney, Congresswoman
Publications: *Ferraro, My Story*
Footnote: Ferraro raised a family, then became an assistant district attorney in Queens, New York. She served in Congress from 1979 to 1985, during which time she was Secretary, Democratic Caucus (1980-84), and Chairman, Democratic Platform Committee (1984). In 1984 Ferraro ran as Democratic candidate for vice-president (with Walter Mondale); the ticket was buried in a Reagan-Bush landslide.

Ella Tambussi Grasso

First Woman to become a state governor in her own right

"I'm having trouble managing the mansion. What I need is a wife."

Born 1919, died 1981
Birthplace: Windsor Locks, Connecticut
Education: Graduated from Mount Holyoke College.
Marital Status/Children: Married Thomas Grasso in 1942; had two children.
Occupation: Public official
Honors: Many awards from Italian-American societies, public service and health organizàtions, religious groups and others
Footnote: During a varied career of public service, Grasso served as a member of the Connecticut General Assembly, as Connecticut Secretary of State (1959-70), and as a Congresswoman (1971-74). In 1975 she began her first term as governor of Connecticut, becoming the first woman to win election as governor who did not follow her husband into office. In 1979, Grasso was re-elected, but died of cancer before completing her second term.

Lorraine Hansberry

First Black Woman to write a play that was produced on Broadway

"The thing I tried to show [in Raisin in the Sun] was the many gradations in even one Negro family, the clash of the old and the new, but most of all the unbelievable courage of the Negro people."

Born 1930, died 1965
Birthplace: Chicago, Illinois
Education: Attended University of Wisconsin
Marital Status/Children: Married Robert Nemiroff, divorced.
Occupation: Playwright
Publications: *To be Young, Gifted and Black* (autobiographical)
Honors: New York Drama Critics Circle Award, 1959
Footnote: Her first play, *Raisin in the Sun,* was a smash hit and became a movie. This play made her the first black and youngest American ever to win the Drama Critics Circle Award. At the time of her death, her second play, *The Sign in Sidney Brustein's Window,* was playing on Broadway.

Patricia Roberts Harris

First Black Woman cabinet member and ambassador

"If my life has any meaning at all, it is that those who start as outcasts may end up being part of the system. I assure you that while there may be those who forget what it meant to be excluded from the dining rooms of this very building [the Capitol], I shall not forget."

Born 1924, died 1985
Birthplace: Mattoon, Illinois
Education: Howard University (BA, 1945), George Washington University Law School (JD, 1960)
Marital Status/Children: Married William Beasley Harris in 1955.
Occupation: Lawyer, government official
Footnote: Harris served under President Carter as both Secretary of Housing and Urban Development (1977-79) and of Health, Education and Welfare (1979-81). Harris was a teacher of law and dean at Howard University Law School, and served as ambassador to Luxembourg (1965-67). As early as 1943 she engaged in a sit-in at a Washington, D.C. cafeteria. She served as a member of the National Commission on the Causes and Prevention of Violence (1969).

Karen Horney

First Freudian psychoanalyst to reject Freud's view that women were disadvantaged because of their anatomy

"The conclusion . . . —that one half of the human race is discontented with the sex assigned to it and can overcome this discontent only in favourable circumstances—is decidedly unsatisfying, not only to feminine narcissism but also to biological science."

Born 1885, died 1952
Birthplace: Eilbek, Germany
Education: Freiburg University, Germany
Marital Status/Children: Married lawyer Oscar Horney, later separated; had 3 daughters.
Occupation: Psychoanalyst
Publications: *New Ways in Psychoanalysis* (1939) and other books
Footnote: After Berlin Psychoanalytic Institute, Horney became assistant director, Chicago Institute of Psychoanalysis. Forced out of NY Psychoanalytic Institute for differing with Freud, Horney founded the Association for the Advancement of Psychoanalysis, the first independent school of psychoanalysis founded by a woman.

Juanita M. Kreps

First Woman Secretary of Commerce

"It is hard to defend the proposition that there are not a great many qualified women (for cabinet positions). . . . We have to do a better job looking."

Born 1921
Birthplace: Lynch, Kentucky
Education: Berea College; Duke University Graduate School (MA and PhD)
Marital Status/Children: Married Clifton Kreps, Jr., in 1944; has two daughters and a son.
Occupation: Professor, academic administrator, economist
Publications: *Sex in the Marketplace: American Women at Work; Lifetime Allocations of Work and Income*
Footnote: Kreps served as Secretary of Commerce under President Carter (1977-1979). She was the first female public director of the New York Stock Exchange, and was Duke University's first woman vice-president. She specializes in problems of economics of the aging and women in the work force, and serves on the boards of several major corporations.

Belva Lockwood

First Woman to be admitted to practice law before the Supreme Court

"I do not believe in sex distinction in literature, law, politics, or trade—or that modesty and virtue are more becoming to women than men."

Born 1830, died 1917
Birthplace: Royalton, New York
Education: Genesee College. The National University Law School refused to admit her in their classes; she was tutored privately and graduated in 1873.
Marital Status/Children: Married Uriah Mcnalls (1848), widowed; married Ezekiel Lockwood (1868); one daughter.
Occupation: Teacher, lawyer, feminist
Publications: Pamphlets on world peace
Honors: Honorary LLD degree from Syracuse University (1909)
Footnote: Lockwood was an effective advocate of women's rights. She secured passage of a law admitting women to practice before the Supreme Court, and helped enact a bill guaranteeing equal pay for equal work for women in the Civil Service. In 1884 and 1888 she ran for president as the National Equal Rights Party candidate.

Clare Booth Luce

First Woman ambassador to a major power

"When an Italian talks with an American he's inclined to feel a twinge of inferiority. America is rich and strong. Italy is poor. But when he talks to me, he's more at ease. I still represent a big, strong nation but I am a woman and he's a man."

Born 1903, died 1987
Birthplace: New York City
Education: Private schools
Marital Status/Children: Married Henry Luce, founder of Time-Life, in 1935, after first marriage dissolved; had one daughter by her first marriage.
Occupation: Magazine editor, playwright, public official, ambassador
Publications: *The Women, Kiss the Boys Goodbye,* and other plays; *Europe in the Spring* and other books
Footnote: A prominent Republican, Luce was the first woman elected to Congress from Connecticut (served 1943-47); was U.S. ambassador to Italy (1953-56) and was, briefly, ambassador to Brazil.

Mary Lyon

First Woman to found a college for women

"My heart has so yearned over the adult female youth in the common walks of life, that it has sometimes seemed as if there was a fire, shut up in my bones."

Born 1797, died 1849
Birthplace: Buckland, Massachusetts
Education: Sanderson Academy; Amherst Academy
Marital Status/Children: Single
Occupation: Teacher, administrator
Publications: *A Missionary Offering,* many pamphlets
Honors: Elected to the Hall of Fame in 1905.
Footnote: In 1834, Mary Lyon began raising funds for Mount Holyoke Female Seminary, which opened its doors on November 8, 1837 in South Hadley, Massachusetts. Lyon's aim was to provide women with the caliber of education available at the finest men's colleges, and one dedicated to Christian principles. Mount Holyoke College (the Seminary's successor) has become one of the leading institutions of higher learning for women.

Wilma Mankiller

First Woman Chief of the Cherokee Nation

"A lot of young girls have looked to their career paths and have said they'd like to be chief. There's been a change in the limits people see."

Born 1945
Birthplace: Stilwell, Oklahoma
Education: Flaming Rainbow College (BA); postgraduate study, University of Arkansas
Marital Status/Children: Married Hector N. Olaya (1953), divorced (1975), 2 children; married Charlie Soap.
Occupation: Chief
Honors: Donnanigh First Lady Award, Oklahoma Commission for Status of Women
Footnote: Mankiller was the first woman deputy chief and the first woman member of the Five Tribes Organization. She presently serves as chief of the second-largest Indian nation in the US, the first woman to do so. Mankiller has promoted small farms, education, jobs, and community and self-help initiatives during her tenure as chief.

Maria Mitchell

First Woman to be elected to the American Academy of Arts and Sciences

"Nature made woman an observer. The schools and schoolbooks have spoiled her."

Born 1818, died 1889
Birthplace: Nantucket, Massachusetts
Education: Nantucket schools, independent study
Marital Status/Children: Single
Occupation: Librarian, astronomer, teacher
Publications: Diaries, lectures, notebooks
Honors: Gold medal from King Christian VIII of Denmark; election to the American Philosophical Society (1869); election to the Hall of Fame (1905)
Footnote: For twenty years Maria Mitchell was a librarian during the day and an astronomer at night. In October, 1847, she discovered the orbit of a new comet, which was subsequently named in her honor. In 1865 she was appointed director of the observatory and professor of astronomy at Vassar College. Mitchell founded the Association for the Advancement of Women.

Constance Baker Motley

First Black Woman Federal Judge and NY State Senator; First Woman NYC Borough President

"A Negro woman lawyer [in the South] is rarer than rare—and they want to see what you're like, how you conduct yourself, how you handle opposing lawyers."

Born: 1921
Birthplace: New Haven, Connecticut
Education: Fiske University and NYU (BA, 1943); Columbia Law School (LLB, 1946)
Marital Status/Children: Married Joel Wilson Motley, 1946; they have a son, Joel.
Occupation: Attorney, legislator, judge
Honors: NY State Bar Association Gold Medal (1988); over 100 civic and professional awards; over 20 honorary degrees.
Footnote: NAACP Legal Defense Fund counsel (1945-1965), Motley has been described as "chief courtroom tactician of the entire civil rights movement." She was the first black woman elected to the NY State Senate (1964), became first female NY City borough president (1965), and was appointed US District Judge (1966). Motley served as Chief Judge, Southern District of New York (1982-86), and assumed Senior District Court Judge status in 1986.

Sandra Day O'Connor

First Woman Justice of the US Supreme Court

"Having family responsibilities and concerns just has to make you a more understanding person."

Born 1930
Birthplace: El Paso, Texas
Education: Stanford University (BA); Stanford Law School (JD)
Marital Status/Children: Married John Jay O'Connor; 3 sons
Occupation: Lawyer, judge
Honors: National Conference of Christians and Jews Award (1975); Disting. Achievement Award, Ariz. State U. (1980)
Footnote: Upon graduation from law school, O'Connor had difficulty finding a job as a lawyer because of the reluctance of law firms to hire a woman. She opened her own law firm in Phoenix and later became an assistant attorney general. After election to the Arizona Senate and service as Superior Court Judge, O'Connor was appointed judge of the Arizona Court of Appeals. In 1981 President Reagan appointed O'Connor to the Supreme Court, where she remains the first and only female to sit on the High Court.

Rosa Parks

First Black Woman to "sit down" for her rights and spark a national civil rights movement

"I'm just an average citizen. Many black people before me were arrested for defying the bus laws. They prepared the way."

Born 1913
Birthplace: Tuskegee, Alabama
Education: High School Graduate
Marital Status/Children: Married Raymond Parks
Occupation: Housekeeper, seamstress, Congressional staffer
Honors: Martin Luther King, Jr., Award (1980)
Footnote: Rosa Parks sparked the Montgomery bus boycott when, on December 1, 1955, after a hard day's work and shopping, she refused to give up her seat to a white man. She was arrested and put in jail. With the backing of Martin Luther King, Jr., the black community, and other supporters, she carried her case to the United States Supreme Court, which ruled a year later against bus company discrimination in a major victory for the civil rights of minorities.

Frances Perkins

First Woman member of the US Cabinet

"Most of man's problems upon this planet, in the long history of the race, have been met and solved either partially or as a whole by experiment based on common sense and carried out with courage."

Born 1882, died 1965
Birthplace: Boston, Massachusetts
Education: Mount Holyoke College graduate; Columbia University (Master's degree)
Marital Status/Children: Married Paul Wilson (1913); had one daughter.
Occupation: Public official, teacher, social worker
Publications: *The Roosevelt I Knew* (1946)
Footnote: Perkins helped to reform working conditions through passage of legislation such as the Social Security Act, Fair Labor Standards Act, and others, as Secretary of Labor for 12 years (1933-45) under President Franklin D. Roosevelt. She also served as executive secretary of the Consumers League of New York, as NYS Industrial Commissioner, and as a member of the US Civil Service Commission (1946-52).

Rabbi Sally Priesand

First Woman Rabbi

"Clergy are father figures to many women, and sometimes they are threatened by another woman accomplishing what they see as strictly male goals. But I can see them replacing that feeling with a sense of pride that women can have that role."

Born 1946
Birthplace: Cleveland, Ohio
Education: University of Cincinnati (BA); Hebrew Union College (MAHL)
Marital Status/Children: Single
Occupation: Rabbi
Publications: *Judaism and the New Woman*
Honors: Honorary degree, Florida International University; Ohio's Outstanding Young Woman of the Year (1972); Eleanor Roosevelt Humanities Award, State of Israel (1980)
Footnote: Priesand, ordained in 1972, was the first female Rabbi in the history of Judaism. She served as assistant rabbi and then associate rabbi at the Stephen Wise Free Synagogue in New York City. At the present time she is the rabbi of Monmouth Reform Temple, Tinton Falls, New Jersey.

Jeannette Rankin

First Woman to be elected to the US House of Representatives

"As a woman I can't go to war, and I refuse to send anyone else."

Born 1880, died 1973
Birthplace: Missoula, Montana
Education: Graduated from University of Montana; attended predecessor of Columbia's New York School of Social Work.
Marital Status/Children: Single
Occupation: Social worker, Congresswoman
Footnote: Jeannette Rankin was a staunch pacifist as well as suffragette. She was the only member of Congress to vote against the entry of the US into World War I. In 1919 Rankin was defeated in her bid for the US Senate, but she continued to work for peace and consumer causes as a lobbyist. She returned to Congress in 1941 and again was the only member of Congress to vote against the US entry into World War II. In 1968, at the age of 88, and still true to the pacifist cause, Rankin led a protest against the Vietnam War on the steps of the Capitol, where she had twice served with distinction.

Linda Richards

First Woman to receive a nursing diploma in the United States

"As for my own work, I often feel that, for the many years I have served, I have accomplished little. Whether I have been a wise builder, someone else must decide."

Born 1841, died 1930
Birthplace: Near Potsdam, New York
Education: Graduated from New England Hospital for Women and Children (1873).
Marital Status/Children: Single
Occupation: Nurse; educator
Honors: Scholarships and awards are named in Richards' honor.
Footnote: Despite the opposition of doctors, Linda Richards developed educational programs for nurses in the US and in Japan. In England, she conferred with Florence Nightingale and studied her methods of training nurses. She was a pioneer in the training of visiting nurses and helped raise the standard of nursing care for the mentally ill.

Ellen H. Swallow Richards

First Woman graduate of MIT; First Woman member of American Institute of Mining and Metallurgical Engineers

"Home life . . . has been robbed by the removal of creative work. You cannot make women contented with cooking and cleaning, and you need not try."

Born 1842, died 1911
Birthplace: Dunstable, Massachusetts
Marital Status/Children: Married MIT Professor Robert H. Richards in 1875.
Education: MIT (BS in Chemistry, 1873) and Vassar College (MA, 1873)
Publications: Books on home economics, chemistry, environment
Honors: First woman elected to AIME; honorary DS from Smith College
Footnote: Admitted to MIT without fee so she would not have to be officially recorded as a student; set up MIT's Women's Laboratory; opened first laboratory in sanitary chemistry (1884); ran Rumford Kitchen at 1893 Chicago World's Fair; founded precursor of American Association of University Women (1908); established home economist and dietitian as professional occupations.

Sally K. Ride

First American Woman astronaut to fly in space

"I didn't come into the space program to be the first woman in space, I came in to get a chance to fly as soon as I could. The thing that I'll remember about the flight is that it was fun."

Born 1951
Birthplace: Encino, California
Education: Stanford University (BS and BA, 1973; PhD, 1978)
Marital Status/Children: Married astronaut Steven A. Hawley, 1982.
Occupation: Astronaut, astrophysicist
Publications: *To Space and Back* (with Susan Okie)
Footnote: In 1978, Sally Ride was chosen by NASA from a pool of 8,000 applicants to become a member of the astronaut program. On June 18, 1983, when the shuttle Challenger lifted off, Ride became the first American woman to go up in space. She was chosen as flight engineer in ascent, reentry, and landing because of her engineering expertise and her ability to get along with others.

Eleanor Roosevelt

"First Lady of the World"

"It's better to light a candle than to curse the darkness."

Born 1884, died 1962
Birthplace: New York City
Education: Schooled in England.
Marital Status/Children: Married Franklin D. Roosevelt 1905; had 5 sons and a daughter.
Occupation: Social worker, teacher, First Lady, columnist, US delegate to the UN.
Publications: Many books and articles; newspaper column "My Day"; *Ladies Home Journal* column
Honors: Repeatedly voted most admired woman in international polls
Footnote: Mrs. Roosevelt held the first press conference by a First Lady (1933). She visited coal mines in the depression, and almost every war front during World War II. As chairman of the UN Commission on Human Rights, Mrs. Roosevelt was instrumental in the adoption in 1948 of the Universal Declaration of Human Rights.

Dr. Florence Sabin

**First Woman elected to the National
Academy of Sciences; First full-time
female professor at medical school;
First female member of the Rockefeller
Institute**

*"If I didn't believe the answer could be found, I
wouldn't be working on it."* [referring to her.
fight against tuberculosis]

Born 1871, died 1953
Birthplace: Central City, Colorado
Education: Graduated from Smith College
(1893) and Johns Hopkins Medical School
(1900).
Marital Status/Children: Single
Occupation: Scientist, anatomist, educator,
writer
Publications: Articles in medical journals,
biography of Frank Pane Mall
Honors: National Achievement Award, the
Trudeau Medal, M. Carey Thomas Prize,
honorary degrees from leading universities
Footnote: One of the first women to enter
medical research, Dr. Sabin made important discoveries concerning lymphatic
vessels, red corpuscles, and tuberculosis.

Muriel Siebert

First Woman to own a seat on the NY Stock Exchange

"Don't take acceptance for granted, or you might end up back in the kitchen."

(Birth date not recorded)
Birthplace: Cleveland, Ohio
Education: Attended Western Reserve University
Marital Status/Children: single
Occupation: Stockbroker
Honors: Honorary degree from St. John's University
Footnote: In 1967, Siebert bought a seat on the NY Stock Exchange for $445,000. She started her own firm in 1969 and in 1975 became one of the first discount brokers. Siebert served as NY State Banking Administrator in the Carey administration from 1977-82, and in 1982 made an unsuccessful bid for the Republican nomination for NY State Senator. She was a co-founder of Women's Forum, an organization of successful women in New York.

Margaret Chase Smith

First Woman to serve in both Houses of Congress

"I don't want to see the Republican Party ride to political victory on the four horsemen of calumny—fear, ignorance, bigotry, and smear."
[on McCarthyism]

Born 1897
Birthplace: Skowhegan, Maine
Education: Skowhegan High School
Marital Status/Children: Married Clyde H. Smith
Occupation: Served as her husband's secretary during his tenure as a Congressman; Congresswoman
Honors: Over 50 honorary degrees and numerous awards; Woman of the Year
Footnote: Upon her husband's death in 1940, Smith was elected to fill his unexpired term in Congress, and was subsequently re-elected to 4 full terms. Smith was then elected to 4 consecutive terms in the Senate (where she served 1949-73). She had one of the best attendance records in Congress, and became the first woman whose name was placed in nomination for the presidency at a national convention of a major party.

Elizabeth Seton

First American Saint

"When so rich a harvest is before us, why do we not gather it? All is in our hands if we will but use it."

Born 1774, died 1821
Birthplace: New York City
Education: Private school
Marital Status/Children: Married William Seton in 1794; five children
Occupation: Nun, educator, social worker
Publications: Many volumes of her writing were presented to Rome in 1914.
Honors: Seton Hall University named in her honor (1856).
Footnote: Elizabeth Seton became a Roman Catholic in 1805. In 1809 she took her vows and within a year organized an order which was later to be called the Sisters of Charity of Saint Joseph. Mother Seton founded St. Joseph College for women, and opened the first free parochial school in the United States. She was beatified in 1963 and canonized in 1975.

Robyn Smith

First Woman jockey to win a major stakes race

"I love horses and speed, and I've always liked competition, but I never knew it would be so satisfying to win. Nothing makes me happier."

Born 1944 (?)
Birthplace: San Francisco, California (?)
Education: Columbia Studio's acting workshop in Hollywood
Marital Status/Children: Married to Fred Astaire, widowed.
Occupation: Jockey
Footnote: Robyn Smith left a promising Hollywood acting career to become a jockey. In a field dominated by men, she surmounted great difficulties, including the unwillingness of owners to give her mounts and other prejudice against women, to rise to the top. In only 4 years at Aqueduct (NY) Race Track, Smith became the fourth-ranked American jockey. Her historic first Stakes win was on March 1, 1973 aboard North Sea. Smith's early life is shrouded in mystery.

Elizabeth Cady Stanton

First president of the National American Woman Suffrage Association

"Social science affirms that a woman's place in society marks the level of civilization."

Born 1815, died 1902
Birthplace: Johnstown, New York
Education: Attended Troy Female Seminary
Marital Status/Children: Married Henry Brewster Stanton in 1840; 7 children.
Occupation: Social reformer
Publications: *The History of Woman Suffrage* (with Susan B. Anthony); *Eighty Years and More* (autobiography, 1898)
Footnote: Stanton was one of the two most important leaders in the women's movement, the other being Susan B. Anthony. Stanton organized the first women's rights convention (Seneca Falls, NY, 1848), with Lucretia C. Mott, and drew up a "Declaration of Sentiments." Stanton led the National Woman Suffrage Association for 20 years, was effective in reforming NY family laws, and became president of the newly-formed National American Woman Suffrage Association in 1890.

Lucy Stone

First Woman in the United States to keep her own name after marriage

" 'We, the people of the United States.' Which 'We, the people'? The women were not included."

Born 1818, died 1893
Birthplace: West Brookfield, Massachusetts
Education: Graduated from Oberlin College (1847)
Marital Status/Children: Married Henry Blackwell in 1855. Had one child, Alice Stone Blackwell, born 1857.
Occupation: Suffragette, Abolitionist
Publications: *Woman's Journal*
Footnote: Stone helped to organize the first national woman's rights convention in 1850 at Worcester, Massachusetts. She founded the American Woman Suffrage Association, an organization which promoted woman suffrage through state legislation. The *Woman's Journal,* which she began in 1872, continued publication until 1917.

Dr. Mary Walker

First Woman to win Medal of Honor

"If men were really what they profess to be they would not compel women to dress so that the facilities for vice would always be so easy."

Born 1832, died 1919
Birthplace: Oswego, New York
Education: Falley Seminary, Syracuse Medical College
Marital Status/Children: Married Dr. Albert Miller (1855), divorced (1869).
Occupation: Surgeon
Publications: *Hit* (1871); *Unmasked, or the Science of Immorality* (1878)
Honors: Won the Army's Medal of Honor for her care of the wounded as an army surgeon on the battlefield in the Civil War.
Footnote: Known for unconventional dress, Walker wore trousers and a long tunic, then an officer's uniform, in the Civil War (during which she was a prisoner of war for 4 months). After the war, in lecturing on women's rights, Dr. Walker wore a man's full evening dress and silk hat. Walker declared: "corsets are coffins."

Sarah Breedlove Walker

First Black Woman millionaire

"America doesn't respect anything but money. You can struggle along sending out teachers, cramming book learning into children that haven't got shoes. What our people need is a few millionaires."

Born 1867, died 1919
Birthplace: Delta, Louisiana
Education: Self-educated
Marital Status/Children: Married Mr. McWilliams, widowed; married C. J. Walker; one daughter
Occupation: Businesswoman
Honors: Named to *Ebony's* "Hall of Fame" of outstanding Negroes.
Footnote: "Madame C. J. Walker" devised a formula for the treatment and straightening of tightly curled hair. Her company employed over 3,000 people, mostly women, many of whom sold and delivered Walker products door-to-door. Walker's successful business enabled her·to give large amounts of money to charity and to educational institutions.

Martha Washington

First "First Lady" of the United States

"I have learned from experience that the greater part of our happiness or misery depends on our dispositions and not on our circumstances."

Born 1731, died 1802
Birthplace: New Kent County, Virginia
Education: No formal education
Marital Status/Children: Married Daniel Parke Custis, 1749, widowed 1757, 4 children. Married George Washington, 1759.
Occupation: First Lady
Footnote: On the death of her first husband, Martha Custis inherited a considerable fortune. In 1759 she married George Washington and moved to Mount Vernon, and in 1789 as First Lady assumed the management of their New York presidential residence. In 1790 the seat of the government moved to Philadelphia, where social gatherings were even more ostentatious than in New York. Although people often referred to Martha Washington as "Lady Washington," guests found her to be gracious and warm.

Victoria Claflin Woodhull

First Woman to be nominated for the presidency of the United States

"All talk of women's rights is moonshine. Women have every right. They have only to exercise them."

Born 1838, died 1927
Birthplace: Homer, Ohio
Education: Self-educated
Marital Status/Children: Married Dr. Canning Woodhull at 15, had two children, divorced in 1864; married Colonel Blood, divorced; married John Martin, 1883.
Occupation: Spiritualist, stockbroker, editor
Publications: *Stirpiculture* (1888); *The Human Body the Temple of God* (1890, co-author); *Humanitarian Money* (1892)
Footnote: Woodhull was born into a poor, eccentric family which toured the Midwest with their medicine and fortune-telling show. In New York, Cornelius Vanderbilt, a fellow believer in spiritualism, set her up as a stockbroker, and she was highly successful. She also published a weekly advocating a single moral standard for men and women. Woodhull became the first woman to be nominated for the presidency, when she ran as the candidate of her own Equal Rights Party.

Jeana Yeager

First Woman Pilot to circle the globe on one tank of gas

"As much as I feared this airplane [the Voyager], I respected it now, and I was proud of it. We had built it, and I felt a oneness with this thing that had carried us so far."

Born 1952(?)
Birthplace: Raised in Texas.
Education: Not known
Marital Status/Children: Divorced, lives with Voyager co-pilot Dick Rutan.
Occupation: Test pilot
Publications: *Voyager* (1988) (Yeager and Rutan with Phil Patton)
Honors: Has set at least 10 aviation speed and endurance records. Received Presidential Citizens Medal.
Footnote: Yeager and Rutan flew the lightweight aircraft *Voyager* around the world in 9 days (December 14-23, 1986) on a single tank of gas, surviving severe storms, technical difficulties, and exhaustion. The cockpit (called a "torture chamber" or a "horizontal telephone booth"), measured 7½' long x 2' x 3' high!

"Babe" Didrikson Zaharias

First Woman of American sports

"I don't seem able to do my best unless I'm behind or in trouble."

Born 1914, died 1956
Birthplace: Port Arthur, Texas
Education: High school graduate
Marital Status/Children: Married wrestler George Zaharias, 1938.
Occupation: Sportswoman; amateur and professional golfer
Publications: *This Life I've Led* (1955), an autobiography
Honors: Outstanding Woman Athlete of the Century (1949 AP Poll)
Footnote: Zaharias won gold medals (and set world records) in the javelin throw and 80-meter hurdles at the1932 Olympics at Los Angeles. She won 17 straight golf tournaments in 1949, and was that year the first American winner of the British Women's Amateur. Incredibly, Zaharias won the 1954 U.S. Open after a cancer operation. In addition to golf, she excelled at baseball, basketball, and billiards.

First Women: American Originators is dedicated to the memory of Edna Beilenson and is in grateful acknowledgment of the critical role that this "first woman" (see page 9) had in the publication of over 500 fine books.

Publication of *First Women: American Originators* marks the 60th anniversary of the Peter Pauper Press. PPP is the product of the efforts of Peter Beilenson, who founded the press in 1928 and was active until 1962, and of Edna Beilenson, who married Peter in 1930 and was intimately involved with Peter Pauper Press as partner and sole owner until 1981. The Press is now under the direction of Evelyn and Nick Beilenson, co-publishers.

Copyright © 1988 Peter Pauper Press, Inc.
ISBN 0-88088-180-1
Library of Congress No. 87-63103
Printed in the United States of America